THIS TREE IS ME

a workbook of self-discovery and career empowerment

Written by Dr. Deanna Behring
Illustrated by Lauren McKee

INTRODUCTION

Have you ever been confused by your various interests? Do you find yourself frustrated and unable to make sense of the opportunities and decisions you face almost daily? Do you want to open up new pathways and consciously create a bright future for yourself? If you answered yes to any of these questions, this book is for you! Together, following my directions, we will create YOUR tree. You will learn about the support structure you have, which is the root system of your tree. Your roots are what keep you firmly planted in life. We will explore what makes you strong, resilient, and unique (the trunk of your tree) and how your various interests (your branches) will grow into a flourishing life and career – your tree.

INTRODUCTION

This workbook grew out of my many experiences with college students who were looking for guidance to help them understand themselves and how their various interests and experiences would lead them to a successful and fulfilling life and career. Many also didn't know how to identify the resources and support network available to them and how to use those resources to get where they wanted to be. Career counselors focus on networking to find a job, and may neglect the deeper work of contributing to the development of the individual as they grow into their fullest potential.

INTRODUCTION

One day, during a particularly complicated conversation with a young student, I pulled out a piece of paper and started drawing what her network would look like and how she could keep track of her network in a way that showcased what it was helping her to create and become. That sketch turned into the beginnings of a tree.

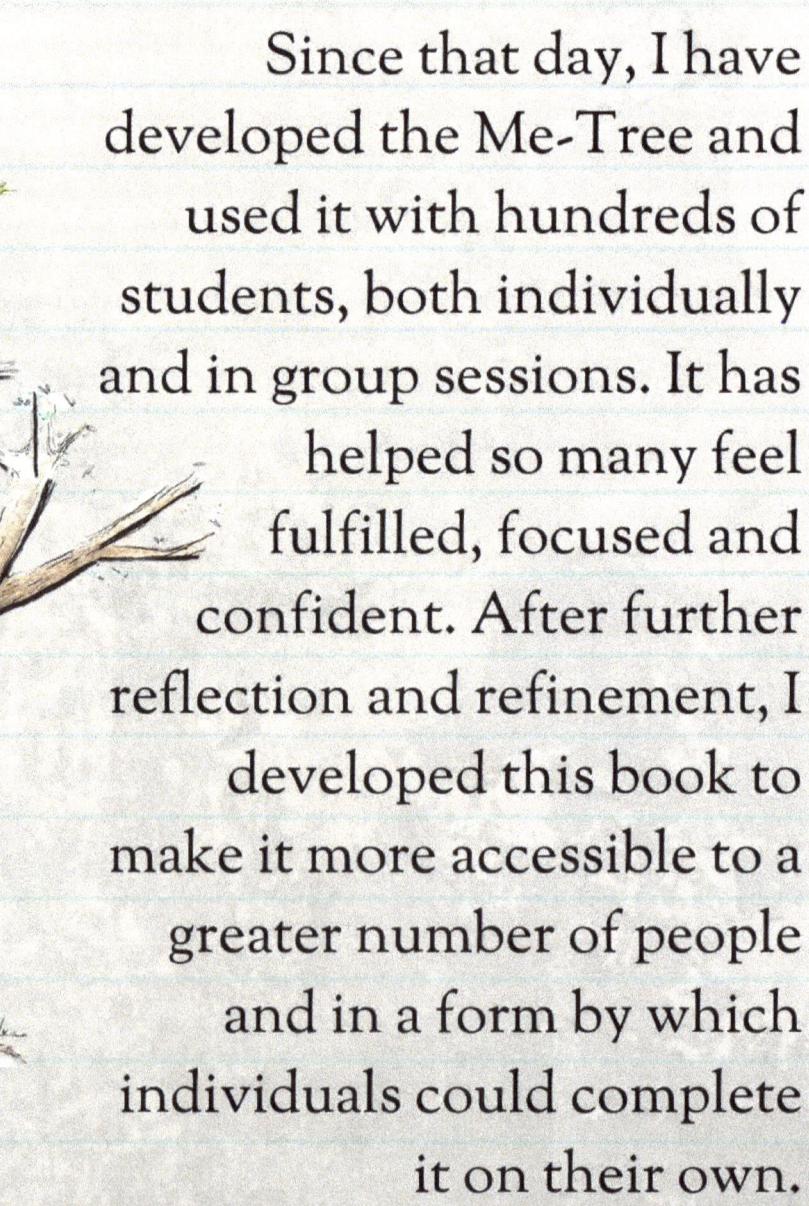

Since that day, I have developed the Me-Tree and used it with hundreds of students, both individually and in group sessions. It has helped so many feel fulfilled, focused and confident. After further reflection and refinement, I developed this book to make it more accessible to a greater number of people and in a form by which individuals could complete it on their own.

WELCOME TO YOUR TREE!

Even before a tree exists, it is an idea, a seed hanging on another branch somewhere, waiting to be carried by the wind or an animal and plant its roots in the soil. Before we bring your tree into existence, take some time to plant some seeds in your imagination. This is a time to reflect on you, what makes you happy, and what is important to you. Be free and creative in your brainstorming. Shake all seeds loose!

Under "Important," write all things that are most important to you. What do you value most in your life? Under "Happy," write all things you do and experience that bring you joy and make you smile. Note that some of these may be the same. That's okay! These reflections will help you define your passion and purpose...they will become key parts of your tree.

MAKE A LIST OF THEM HERE:

HAPPY

_____
_____
_____
_____
_____
_____
_____
_____
_____
_____

IMPORTANT

_____
_____
_____
_____
_____
_____
_____
_____
_____
_____

Now that you have named your tree, it's time to think about your roots—what keeps your tree firmly planted?

- Who or what supports you?
- Who or what is important to you and makes you happy?

Think of this as your support structure. Your roots are made up of fundamental values, people who have been instrumental in your learning, philosophies you admire, people who you can consult, networks and skills you have developed, strengths you have which you value. You can always come back and add more later.

MAKE A LIST OF THEM HERE:

_____ _____ _____
_____ _____ _____
_____ _____ _____
_____ _____ _____

Think about your favorite tree from your childhood. Did you have one that you were able to climb or sit under or just look at? Do you remember how their branches looked? Go for a walk or look out your window to find one.

Look at how the trunk divides into branches...big ones at first, growing smaller and smaller as they fill out the tree and grow leaves. Maybe some fare better than others. Or, maybe one branch gets damaged and comes to an end. But notice that even when that happens, the tree lives on through its other branches. This is like your tree. Your tree is an ecosystem that includes your support system (roots) and your interests and avenues (branches). You can look at your tree and trust that as you move through your career and life, some of the branches may fall away. That's okay! You have other means of support. Sometimes, releasing what is not meant to be can help the other branches grow stronger. There are always other avenues and branches. As we create your tree on the next few pages, you will be able to see how many options you have.

Creating your main branches may be the hardest part of this process as you try to define your main interests and motivators. Each main branch will represent one of those main interests of yours. Reflect back to what is most important to you and how that manifests in a life goal or career interest.

To help discern between your main interests and your side interests, ask yourself:

- What excites you?
- What do you value most?
- What is important to you as you think about creating your future?

IT'S YOUR TURN!

Pick how many branches you want to start with and fill them in on this page. If many interests come to mind, just pick a few for now. You can always return to this workbook at any time. As you grow and change, so can your tree.

Now, let's take one main branch at a time and start creating new offshoots. These new offshoots represent ways to realize your main interests. They can be the places or organizations you admire, the ideas you want to experiment with, or the things you want to learn more about.

You can choose the number of initial offshoots you want, but try to stay focused and "shoot" for three! We will be building your action plan from these initial offshoots in the pages ahead.

Now you get to see your tree start to come to life as your initial offshoots lead to additional branches representing your action plan(s). Reflect back on your favorite childhood tree. Recall how each branch supports a number of additional branches. Use this space here to draw two secondary branches from your initial offshoots. Each of these secondary branches should represent actions you can take to advance your main interests: training or classes you can take, people you can talk to, or jobs you can apply for. You can continue this process as long as you want as new actions lead to new opportunities. Eventually, you will have a complete tree that represents you, your core values, and the support systems and opportunities you can use to realize your full potential.

Here is an example to use as a model.

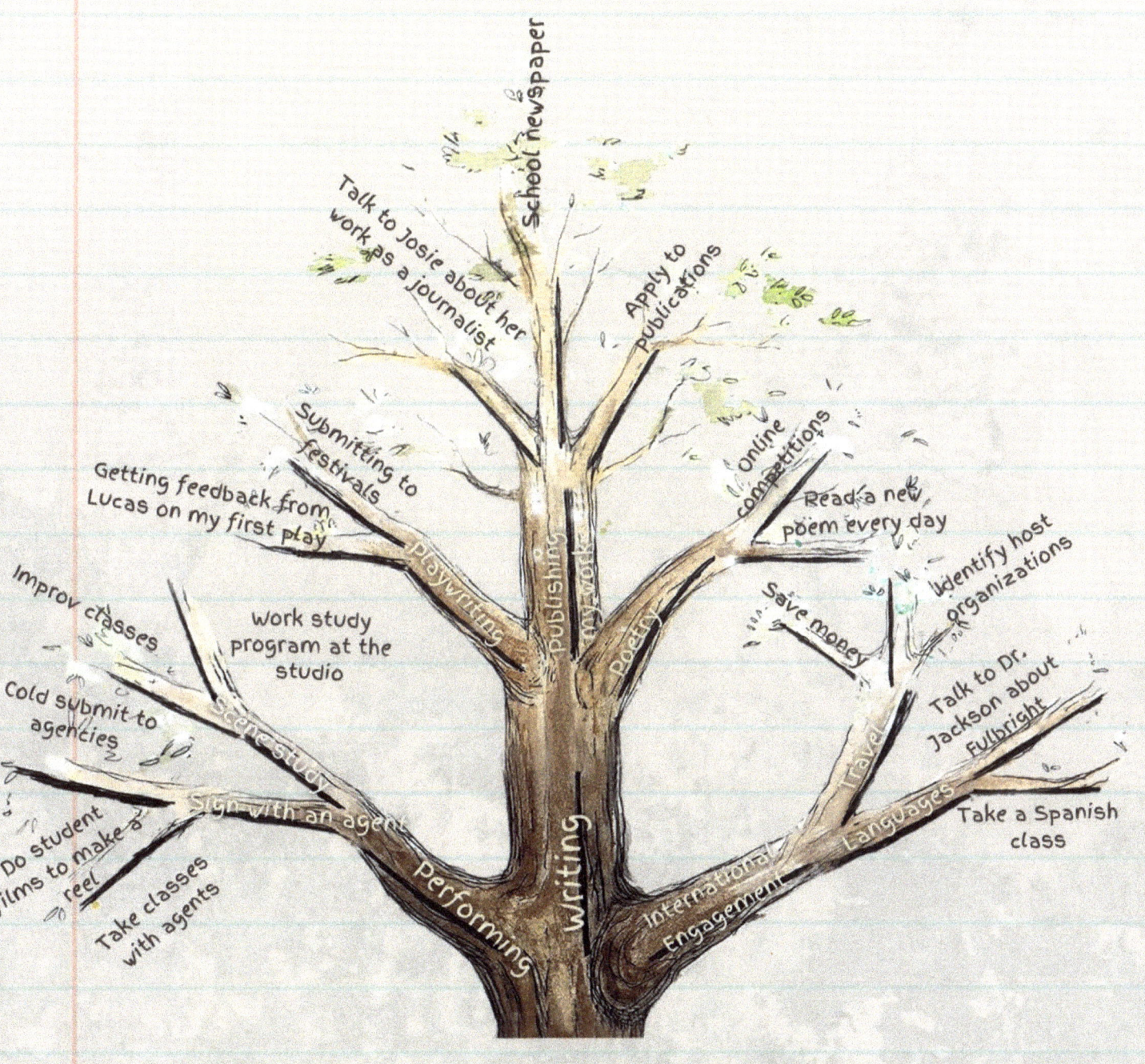

Now, it's your turn to create your action plan.

IT'S TIME TO BE CREATIVE!

Fill in your tree with all the components.

Grab your favorite colors and draw in the leaves, the fruit, and any animals that might want to live in your tree. Notice how full of life your tree has become. Make sure to leave room for further growth and new opportunities in the future!

CONGRATULATIONS!

You have thought a lot about yourself and have completed your tree! Keep this tree near you. Rip out page 19 and put it in a place of honor. Pick somewhere special where you will see it periodically. You can revisit your tree when you need it most to remind yourself of what you care about, what keeps you grounded, and the steps you are taking to realize the fullest version of you.

Finally, remember that trees are resilient to change and injury. If one branch doesn't keep growing for whatever reason, it doesn't mean the tree stops growing. The tree draws on its roots to keep its trunk strong and to help other branches thrive. This is also you.

EPILOGUE

I hope you've benefited from this exercise and a different way to think about your career planning and life goals. I find the tree drawing to be useful on several fronts. It is not only an artistic way to present and organize information, but also a symbol to remind us of our connectivity, to ourselves and to our community and our world.

Trees show up throughout history and in a variety of religions and philosophies as metaphors for the human being. The Jewish calendar reserves one day each year, the "New Year for Trees" on the 15th of Shevat, for us to contemplate our affinity with the botanical universe. The Torah compares us to trees, because a human being is also comprised of three components: roots, a body, and fruit.

EPILOGUE

This comparison holds true on three levels: psychologically, chronologically and spiritually. The "Tree of Life" symbolism has also become more commonplace and you will often see it in art or in jewelry, as pendants on necklaces. The Tree of Life has a long history, crossing many cultures. For our purposes in this workbook, we approached the tree as a symbol of your growth into a beautiful and unique person. When trees are young, they pretty much all look the same. But, as they grow older, they weather storms and are battered by the forces of wind and water. Their branches may break and grow back in a different direction, or the very soil beneath them will erode away, causing them to grow even stronger roots to hold on. They become unique and beautiful in their individuality... just like you!

NOTES

Praise for This Tree is Me:

In this world of overwhelming options and choices, Dr. Behring's tree method provided me with refreshing clarity. This method allowed me to visualize and solidify my desires and goals for my career and helped me to identify my current role – a position which has proven to be a dream job. This plan is a straightforward tool to help anyone wrestling with options and trying to determine the best direction to move in their career and personal life.
   -Noel Habashy, Assistant Professor, Penn State

The tree career planning process is a refreshingly simple approach to mapping interests and goals. Wherever you are in your job search or your professional journey, the career planning tree will add clarity to both ambitions that are familiar and those not before articulated.
–Taylor Grove, School of International Affairs, Penn State

ABOUT THE AUTHOR

The author brings a variety of career experiences to create this book, as you would hope! Dr. Deanna Behring received her PhD in Communications at age 51 while working full time and raising two really cool daughters. Dr. Behring currently serves as Assistant Dean of International Programs at Penn State University and loves her students and the opportunity to share the "Tree" with all of them. Prior to joining Penn State, Dr. Behring worked for the Central Intelligence Agency, the White House Office of Science and Technology Policy under President Clinton, and spent several years working in international development to advance maternal and child health in countries around the world. She also speaks French and Chinese. All of these experiences have grown out of her main tree branches: her interest in using international and multicultural engagement to make the world a better place.

ABOUT THE ILLUSTRATOR

Lauren McKee is a Penn State student working on her Art History degree and Museum Studies certificate with an internship at the Palmer Museum of Art. She will finish her BFA in Acting next year. Lauren has loved illustrating since childhood and is grateful to be a part of this project!

ABOUT THE EDITOR

Kait Warner is an actor and writer based in NYC. She has worked in cast and creative Off-Broadway, and is currently writing a commissioned musical and a play set to perform at the 2021 Edinburgh Fringe Festival. Always looking to connect with new people and experiences, Kait enjoys learning new instruments and languages. She holds a BFA from NYU Tisch Drama and a minor in Creative Writing.

© 2021 Deanna Behring

Printed in the United States of America

All rights reserved. This publication is protected by Copyright, and permission should be obtained from the publisher prior to any prohibited reproduction, storage in a retrieval system, or transmission in any form or by any means, electronic, mechanical, photocopying, recording, or likewise.

Published by Berry St. Books, an imprint of Eifrig Publishing,
PO Box 66, Lemont, PA 16851, USA
Knobelsdorffstr. 44, 14059 Berlin, Germany.

For information regarding permission, write to:
Rights and Permissions Department,
Eifrig Publishing,
PO Box 66, Lemont, PA 16851, USA.
permissions@eifrigpublishing.com, +1-814-954-9445

Library of Congress Cataloging-in-Publication Data
Behring, Deanna
This Tree is Me: /
by Deanna Behring, illustrated by Lauren McKee

p. cm.

Paperback: ISBN978-1-63233-288-2
Ebook: ISBN 978-1-63233-289-9

[1. Self-help . 2. Career planning]
I. McKee, Lauren. , ill. II. Title: This Tree is Me

25 24 23 22 2021
5 4 3 2 1

Printed on recycled acid-free paper. ∞

www.ingramcontent.com/pod-product-compliance
Lightning Source LLC
Chambersburg PA
CBHW040013080526
44586CB00028B/2990